TONI MORRISON

Remember

The Journey to School Integration

 HOUGHTON MIFFLIN COMPANY ★ BOSTON 2..

D1533768

⌐⌐⌐

The captions included in this book are not intended to be the actual thoughts of
the people in the photographs. Rather, they represent the author's notion of what
an individual in the position depicted might have been thinking. Whatever views
these individuals may have held at the time may well be different today.

www.houghtonmifflinbooks.com

The text of this book was set in Legacy.
The title type was set in P22 Monet.

Library of Congress Cataloging-in-Publication Data

Morrison, Toni.
Remember : the journey to school integration / by Toni Morrison.
p. cm.
ISBN 0-618-39740-X
1. School integration—United States—Pictorial works.
2. Discrimination in education—United States—Pictorial works.
3. African Americans—Education—Pictorial works. 4. United
States—Race relations—Pictorial works. I. Title.
LC214.2.M67 2004
379.2'63'0222—dc22
2003022884

Manufactured in the United States of America
WOZ 10 9 8 7 6 5 4 3 2 1

Design by Sheila Smallwood

The Narrow Path, the Open Gate, the Wide Road

*T*his book is about you. Even though the main event in the story took place many years ago, what happened before it and after it is now part of all our lives. Because remembering is the mind's first step toward understanding, this book is designed to take you on a journey through a time in American life when there was as much hate as there was love; as much anger as there was hope; as many heroes as cowards. A time when people were overwhelmed with emotion and children discovered new kinds of friendships and a new kind of fear. As with any journey, there is often a narrow path to walk before you can see the wide road ahead. And sometimes there is a closed gate between the path and the road.

To enliven the trip, I have imagined the thoughts and feelings of some of the people in the photographs chosen to help tell this story. They are children, teenagers, adults; ordinary people leading ordinary lives all swept up in events that would mark all of our lives.

The first people to step onto the long path were children and their parents. The laws in many states, called Jim Crow laws, demanded separation of the races in all public places and especially the public schools. These laws were based on the idea of "separate but equal." That meant black people could enter public areas, use public facilities such as drinking fountains and waiting rooms in train stations, be seated on public transportation, go to parks and movie theaters, and attend schools, but not with white people.

Sitting apart on a bus or not being served through the front window of a takeout restaurant was humiliating, but nothing was more painful than being refused a decent education. No matter how much they argued or how long they complained, black families had to send their children to all-black schools, no matter how far away. Many buildings were dilapidated, even dangerous. Textbooks were few, worn, and out of date; there

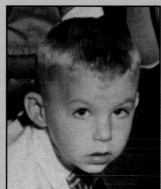

were no supplies, no after-school programs, school lunches, sports equipment. Underpaid teachers were overburdened trying to make do. Then one day, some parents from Delaware, Kansas, South Carolina, Virgina, and Washington, D.C., stepped onto the path. These African American parents formed a group represented by lawyers for the NAACP (National Association for the Advancement of Colored People) to sue school boards that required their children to travel to schools miles away from white ones closer to their homes. Their case was named for one of the parents, Oliver Brown, who was part of the Kansas group.

The closed gates were opened by the Supreme Court after many lawyers and thousands of people pushed against them. On May 17, 1954, the Supreme Court justices announced a decision in the case of *Brown v. Board of Education*. The decision, which said separate schools were not equal, threw many states, cities, towns, neighborhoods, principals, teachers, parents, and students into confusion. Battles were fought to honor, ignore, or overturn the decision. Many battles were won, some quietly, some not.

The demand to integrate public schools grew into a nationwide civil rights movement to eliminate all racist law: to have the right to vote, the right to choose the neighborhood you wanted to live in, to sit in any vacant seat in a public place. Marches, protests, countermarches, and counterprotests erupted almost everywhere. It was an extraordinary time, when people of all races and all walks of life came together. When children had to be braver than their parents, when pastors, priests, and rabbis left their altars to walk the streets with strangers, when soldiers with guns were assigned to keep the peace or to protect a young girl. Days full of loud, angry, determined crowds, and days deep in loneliness. Peaceful marches were met with applause in some places, violence in others. People were hurt and people died. Students and civil rights workers were hosed, beaten, jailed. Strong leaders were shot and killed. And one day a bomb was thrown into a church, killing four little girls attending Sunday school.

None of that happened to you. Why offer memories you do not have? Remembering can be painful, even frightening. But it can also swell your heart and open your mind.

Whenever I see sheets drying on the line or smell gumbo simmering on the stove, a flood of memories comes back to me. In 1953 when I traveled in the rural South with a group of students, we received the generosity of strangers—African Americans who took us in when there were no places for nonwhites to eat or sleep. They were strangers who gave up their own beds, dressed them in brilliant white linen smelling of mulberry and pine. They fed us from their gardens and were so insistent on not being paid, we had to hide money in the pillow slips so they would find it long after we were gone. These were country people, or city people denied adequate education, relegated to a tiny balcony area in a movie theater, backs of buses and separate water fountains, menial jobs or none. Like me, they were ordinary people. Yet, although their lives were driven by laws that said, "No, not here," "No, not there," "No, not you," racial segregation had not marked their souls.

The joy I felt in 1954, when the Supreme Court decided the *Brown v. Board of Education* case, was connected to those generous strangers, and even now wind-dried sheets can summon up my memory of what that decision did and what it meant for all our futures. This book is a celebration of the power and justice of that decision.

So remember. Because you are a part of it. The path was not entered, the gate was not opened, the road was not taken only for those brave enough to walk it. It was for you as well. In every way, this is your story.

The Narrow Path

Years ago, children of different races could not go to school together in many places in the United States. School districts could legally segregate students into different schools according to the color of their skin. The law said these separate schools had to be equal. However, many schools for children of color were inferior to the schools for white students.

The law says I can't go to school with white children. Are they afraid of my socks, my braids? I am seven years old. Why are they afraid of me?

Her name was Betty when she belonged to my cousin. Then her name was Alice when my sister got her. Now she's mine and I call her Jasmine. I think her dress was red with white dots and I remember she had a white underslip with lace, and panties too. They got torn and thrown away. She can't cry Mama anymore. All she has now is yellow hair and green eyes. I like playing with her. She doesn't stick out her tongue or call me names. And she doesn't hide behind her mother's dress, pointing at me, when I go into town. She's a good friend, my Jasmine.

*O*utside the grass is tall and full of bees and butterflies. The peaches that fall off the trees split sometimes and the juice is sweeter than cake. In here I am supposed to learn important things. I bet I could be good at learning them if I had a real desk and lots of books and things. I want to. But it's dark in here. Outside the sky is blue and the peaches are sweeter than cake.

Our parents sued the Board of Education not because they hate them, but because they love us. They are full of hope but they are determined, too. No matter how narrow the path or how long the journey, all of us are on it together.

The Open Gate

On May 17, 1954, the U.S. Supreme Court announced a decision that changed the way students went to school. At the end of the *Brown v. Board of Education* case, the Supreme Court declared that "separate educational facilities are inherently unequal." The case changed the law so that schools could no longer be segregated. Supreme Court Justice Frankfurter wrote that it was "a day that will live in glory." For many people, the decision did make May 17, 1954, a glorious day, but not for everyone. When the new school year began in the autumn of 1954, some students went to school together who never had before. But in many places, people resisted the Supreme Court ruling.

"All the News That's Fit to Print"

The New York Times.

LATE CITY EDITION
Fair and cool today. Mostly sunny, continued cool tomorrow.
Temperature Range Today—Max., 65; Min., 52
Temperatures Yesterday—Max., 69; Min., 61
Full U. S. Weather Bureau Report, Page 31

Copyright, 1954, by The New York Times Company.

VOL. CIII....No. 35,178. Entered as Second-Class Matter, Post Office, New York, N. Y. NEW YORK, TUESDAY, MAY 18, 1954. Times Square, New York 36, N. Y. Telephone Lackawanna 4-1000 FIVE CENTS

HIGH COURT BANS SCHOOL SEGREGATION; 9-TO-0 DECISION GRANTS TIME TO COMPLY

McCarthy Hearing Off a Week as Eisenhower Bars Report

SENATOR IS IRATE

President Orders Aides Not to Disclose Details of Top-Level Meeting

President's letter and excerpts from transcript, Pages 24, 25, 26.

By W. H. LAWRENCE
Special to The New York Times.

WASHINGTON, May 17—A secrecy directive by President Eisenhower resulted today in an abrupt recess for at least a week of the Senate's Army-McCarthy hearings.

Democratic and Republican Senators, some publicly and some privately, predicted that the investigation might never resume in earnest. However, there were other Senators who insisted that the investigation would go on to completion.

The recess was voted after Herbert Brownell Jr., the Attorney General, disclosed formally that criminal prosecutions might be instituted against those involved in the "preparation and dissemination" of an altered, condensed but still confidential Federal Bureau of Investigation report. This was offered in evidence last week by Senator Joseph R. McCarthy, Republican of Wisconsin.

Republicans outvoted Democrats 4 to 3 on the Senate Permanent Subcommittee of Investigation to recess the hearings until 10 o'clock next Monday morning. They acted amid charges and denials that the way was being prepared for a "whitewash."

Constitutional Division Cited

President Eisenhower cited the constitutional separation of powers between the Executive and Legislative branches in directing that details and conversations at a "high level" Administration meeting on Jan. 21 must be withheld from the committee.

Testimony already has been given that top White House, Justice and Defense officials had made plans at that conference to deal with Senator McCarthy.

The Presidential order served effectively to seal the lips of John G. Adams, the Army's regular counselor, about what Sherman Adams, the chief Presidential assistant, said to him in advising that a written report be prepared on how Senator McCarthy and his chief counsel, Roy M. Cohn, persistently sought preferential treatment for Pvt. G. David

Communist Arms Unloaded in Guatemala By Vessel From Polish Port, U. S. Learns

State Department Views News Gravely Because of Red Infiltration

Special to The New York Times.

WASHINGTON, May 17—The State Department said today that it had reliable information that "an important shipment of arms" had been sent from Communist-controlled territory to Guatemala.

It said the arms, now being unloaded at Puerto Barrios, Guatemala, had been shipped from Stettin, a former German Baltic seaport, which has been occupied by Communist Poland since World War II. The Guatemalan regime has been frequently accused of being influenced by Communists.

"Because of the origin of these arms, the point of their embarkation, their destination and the quantity of arms, involved, the Department of State considers that this is a development of gravity," the announcement said.

A freighter arrived at Puerto

Gulf of
Mexico
MEXICO
Caribbean
Sea
BRITISH HONDURAS
GUATEMALA
Puerto Barrios
HONDURAS
Guatemala
EL SALVADOR
NICAR.

The New York Times May 18, 1954
Site of arms arrival (cross)

Embassy Says Nation of Central America May Buy Munitions Anywhere

Barrios last Saturday, the State Department reported, carrying a large shipment of armament consigned to the Guatemalan Government.

The State Department did not divulge the exact quantity of the arms, their nature or where they had been manufactured.

Reliable sources told The New York Times, however, that ten freight car loads of goods listed in the manifest as "hardware" had been unloaded from this ship and sent to the city of Guatemala since Sunday. Guatemala is 150 miles from Puerto Barrios. The

Continued on Page 10, Column 5

SOVIET BIDS VIENNA CEASE 'INTRIGUES'

Envoy Warns Austrian Chief on Inciting East Zone—Raab Denies Charges

By JOHN MacCORMAC
Special to The New York Times.

VIENNA, May 17—The Soviet Union warned Austria today to put an end to "hostile and subversive intrigues" against the Soviet occupation forces, or Soviet authorities would do it themselves.

Ivan I. Ilyichev, Soviet High Commissioner, reverted to a practice of early post-war days by summoning Chancellor Julius Raab and Vice Chancellor Adolf Schaerf to give them this warning. The Chancellor denied the Soviet charges.

Mr. Ilyichev said the Austrian Government had been guilty of staging actions hostile to the Soviet while the Austrian press had published daily slanderous and inciting announcements about the Soviet Union and Soviet occupation troops.

The cessation of Soviet control over the movement of freight, said the High Commissioner, was abused to smuggle militarist literature and provocative incitements into the Soviet zone with the connivance of the Austrian Minister of Interior.

City Colleges' Board Can't Pick Chairman

The Board of Higher Education was unable to elect a chairman at its annual meeting last night at Hunter College.

A spokesman said it was the first time "within memory of board officials" that such a situation had occurred.

Nineteen of the twenty-one members of the board, which governs the four municipal colleges, attended.

Two members nominated for the one-year-term were unable to attain the required majority of eleven votes. They were Joseph B. Cavallaro, who was up for re-election as chairman, and Dr. Harry J. Carman, who was restored to the board on March 2 by Mayor Wagner.

The election was laid over until June 15.

INDO-CHINA PARLEY WEIGHS TWO PLANS

French and Rebel Peace Bids Will Be Studied Jointly as a Basis for Settlement

By THOMAS J. HAMILTON
Special to The New York Times.

GENEVA, May 17—The Far East conference decided today to

2 TAX PROJECTS DIE IN ESTIMATE BOARD

Beer Levy and More Parking Collections Killed—Payroll Impost Still Weighed

By CHARLES G. BENNETT

Two possible new revenue sources were definitely eliminated yesterday by the Board of Estimate in executive session. They were the proposed 1-cent-a-glass tax on beer and the suggestion to extend metered parking into hours now "free."

In a three-hour City Hall parley the board failed once more to decide on a new impost or imposts to balance the 1954-55 budget of $1,639,438,325. Mayor Wagner said after the meeting that the highly controversial 3 per cent sales tax on commercial services was "still one of the taxes at the top of the list."

Saying he felt the Board of Estimate was close to a decision on the knotty tax question, the Mayor added that "there's no decision to discard any tax" except the two mentioned above, and that at the same time "no tax is inevitable."

The board will wrestle with the tax question again in executive session on Thursday at 2:30 P. M. The Mayor said the City Council, which is holding up a bill to impose the sales tax extension, would be invited to send

REACTION OF SOUTH

'Breathing Spell' for Adjustment Tempers Region's Feelings

By JOHN N. POPHAM
Special to The New York Times.

CHATTANOOGA, Tenn., May 17—The South's reaction to the Supreme Court's decision outlawing racial segregation in public schools appeared to be tempered considerably today.

The time lag allowed for carrying out the required transitions seemed to be the major factor in that reaction.

Southern leaders of both races in political, educational and community service fields expressed comment that covered a wide range. Some spoke bitter words that verged on defiance. Others ranged from sharp disagreement to predictions of peaceful and successful adjustment in accord with the ruling.

But underneath the surface of much of the comment, it was evident that many Southerners recognized that the decision had laid down the legal principle rejecting segregation in public education facilities.

They also noted that it had left open a challenge to the region to join in working out a program of necessary changes in the present bi-racial school systems.

Three of the most illustrative viewpoints were those expressed by Govs. James F. Byrnes of South Carolina and Herman Talmadge of Georgia, and Harold Fleming, a spokesman for the Southern Regional Council, the most effective interracial organization in the South.

Byrnes Sees Reversal

Governor Byrnes, who has vigorously defended the doctrine of separate but equal facilities in education, said that he was "shocked to learn that the court has reversed itself" with regard to past rulings on that doctrine.

However, Governor Byrnes, a former Associate Justice of the Supreme Court, noted that the tribunal had not yet delivered its final decree setting forth the time and terms for ending segregation in the schools.

Pointing out that South Carolina, a party in the litigation before the court, had until October to present arguments on how the Supreme Court should order the implementation of the decision, Governor Byrnes declared "I urge all of our people, white and colored, to exercise restraint and preserve order."

Associated Press Wirephoto
LEADERS IN SEGREGATION FIGHT: Lawyers who led battle before U. S. Supreme Court for abolition of segregation in public schools congratulate one another as they leave court after announcement of decision. Left to right: George E. C. Hayes, Thurgood Marshall and James M. Nabrit.

MORETTIS' LAWYER MUST BARE TALKS

Jersey Court Orders Counsel to Racketeers in Bergen to Divulge Data to Grand Jury

By GEORGE CABLE WRIGHT
Special to The New York Times.

TRENTON, May 17—The New Jersey Supreme Court today ordered a lawyer who once had represented top Bergen County racketeers to divulge to a grand jury the substance of confidential talks with those clients.

The four-to-three decision reversed the rulings of two lower courts. Involved was the refusal more than a year ago of John E. Selser, Hackensack attorney, to answer four questions put to him by the Bergen County grand jury.

Mr. Selser told the jury that one of his clients, Willie Moretti, slain gambler, had given him the names of persons connected with

RULING TO FIGURE IN '54 CAMPAIGN

Decision Tied to Eisenhower—Russell Leads Southerners in Criticism of Court

By WILLIAM S. WHITE
Special to The New York Times.

WASHINGTON, May 17—Congress as a whole grappled gingerly today with the profound political implications of the Supreme Court's anti-segregation decision.

It became clear at once—and by both parties was accepted in private as inevitable—that the court's action would figure importantly in the coming Congressional election campaigns.

Publicly, however, the Republicans and the non-Southern Democrats on the whole maintained silence. The Southerners, all angry or sorrowing in one degree or another, were quickly articulate and split among themselves

1896 RULING UPSET

'Separate but Equal' Doctrine Held Out of Place in Education

Text of Supreme Court decision is printed on Page 15.

By LUTHER A. HUSTON
Special to The New York Times.

WASHINGTON, May 17—The Supreme Court unanimously outlawed today racial segregation in public schools.

Chief Justice Earl Warren read two opinions that put the stamp of unconstitutionality on school systems in twenty-one states and the District of Columbia where segregation is permissive or mandatory.

The court, taking cognizance of the problems involved in the integration of the school systems concerned, put over until the next term, beginning in October, the formulation of decrees to effectuate its 9-to-0 decision.

The opinions set aside the "separate but equal" doctrine laid down by the Supreme Court in 1896.

"In the field of public education," Chief Justice Warren said, "the doctrine of 'separate but equal' has no place. Separate educational facilities are inherently unequal."

He stated the question and supplied the answer as follows:

"We come then to the question presented: Does segregation of children in public schools solely on the basis of race, even though physical facilities and other 'tangible' factors may be equal, deprive the children of the minority group of equal educational opportunities? We believe that it does."

States Stressed Rights

The court's opinion does not apply to private schools. It is directed entirely at public schools. It does not affect the "separate but equal doctrine" as applied on railroads and other public carriers entirely within states that have such restrictions.

The principal ruling of the court was in four cases involving state laws. The states' right to operate separated schools had been argued before the court on two occasions by representatives of South Carolina, Virginia, Kansas and Delaware.

In these cases, consolidated in one opinion, the high court held that school segregation deprived Negroes of "the equal protection of the laws guaranteed by the Fourteenth Amendment."

1 think she likes me, but how can I tell? What will I do if she hates me?

$\mathcal{G}$reat! Now we can have some fun!

I don't know. My buddies talked me into this. They said it would be fun. It's not, but these guys are my friends and friends are more important than strangers. Even if they're wrong. Aren't they?

*W*hen they let us in the school, none of the white students came. Their parents made them stay home.

No, no, they said. You can't come in here. Get away from the door. This school is for white children. Only them.

$\mathcal{W}$alking through a crowd of people who hate what we are—not what we do—can make us hate them back for what they are and what they do. A lot of courage and determination are needed not to. We try . . .

but sometimes . . .

Soldiers with rifles stop me. Who knows? Will they shoot me if I don't obey?

I eat alone. No one looks at me. I can't (won't) look at them.

$\mathcal{T}$hey told me and my sister to get off the sidewalk. I made them do it instead.

I see in her face just a girl. She sees in my face another girl. Maybe not friends, but simply girls together.

They are trying to scare me. I guess they don't have any children of their own. But didn't grownups used to be little kids who knew how it felt to be scared?

1 can't see anything but the dark inside the door. My father is strong and smart. He holds my hand in his big fist. When he leaves me here I'll have to be strong too. I can do it. I know I can, even though all I can see in front of me now is the dark.

The Wide Road

In communities all over the United States,

the idea of separate but equal applied to much more than

schools. There were segrated restaurants and water fountains.

There were separate sections in movie theaters and on buses and

trains for people of different races. African American people had

difficulty voting, buying homes, and getting good jobs. Many

black citizens, with white supporters, became part of a

movement to demand equality and civil rights.

1 know the water I am drinking at this fountain is the same as the water over there. The whites know it too. Seems foolish but it's not. It's important if you want to make a grown man feel small. It's extra work and costs more money to have two fountains when one will do, and to pretend water cares who's drinking it. But I guess some folks will do anything to make themselves feel big.

SAENGER
Colored
Entrance

ADMISSION
10¢

SAENGER
▾ COLORED ENTRANCE ▾

NOW PLAYING

OUT WEST WITH
THE HARDYS

STONE
ROONEY
PARKER
HOLDEN

NOW PLAYING

LEWIS STONE
MICKEY ROONEY
CECILIA PARKER
FAY HOLDEN

INSURANCE

This isn't easy, sitting here so everybody can see you and know right away which side you're on. It's such a simple thing: go into a public place, sit down, and try to order a cup of coffee or a soda pop. Nothing more normal. Except when there are laws and people who don't want you to. I'm sure they won't win in the long run; not if plain people like us are willing to object. Still, it's not all that easy. You can feel the eyes, the silence, the hate. What makes it worth it is we are going to change things; what helps is doing it with a friend.

Some people marched and fought and worked hard to end segregation.

$\mathcal{O}$thers smashed eggs on our heads and threw water in our faces.

1 am not confused. I don't want to be treated as *though* I am equal, but *because* I am.

I've never been arrested or jailed before. I'm scared but not afraid . . .

. . . because if I ever feel helpless or lonely I just have to remember that sometimes all it takes is one person.

$\mathcal{T}$hen the loneliness melts away.

1 am drawing a Magic Man. He can make anything happen. Anything at all. Just wait and see.

Anything can happen. Anything at all. See?

This book is dedicated to

Denise McNair, Carole Robertson, Addie Mae Collins, and Cynthia Wesley,
who died in the racist bombing of their Birmingham church on
September 15, 1963.

Things are better now.
Much, much better.
But remember why and please
remember us.

Their lives short, their deaths quick.
Neither were in vain.

KEY EVENTS IN CIVIL RIGHTS AND SCHOOL INTEGRATION HISTORY

1896 — The U.S. Supreme Court legalizes separate but equal facilities in *Plessy v. Ferguson*.

1935 — The NAACP launches a legal campaign against segregation.

1950–1951 — The NAACP lawyers file five lawsuits challenging school segregation. These cases go to the Supreme Court as *Brown v. Board of Education* in 1952.

MAY 17, 1954 — The U.S. Supreme Court declares segregated schools unconstitutional in *Brown v. Board of Education*.

DECEMBER 1955 — Rosa Parks refuses to give her seat to a white passenger on a Montgomery, Alabama, city bus. This incident leads to the Montgomery bus boycott.

SEPTEMBER 1957 — The Arkansas National Guard prevents nine black students from enrolling in school in Little Rock. President Eisenhower sends federal troops to enforce desegregation.

FEBRUARY 1960 — Four black college students stage a sit-in to protest a whites-only lunch counter in Greensboro, North Carolina.

NOVEMBER 1960 — Ruby Bridges and three other first-graders integrate the New Orleans public schools.

MAY 1961 — Freedom Riders face attacks and prison as they try to integrate interstate buses.

MAY 1963 — Two thousand children go to jail in Birmingham, Alabama, for marching in the Children's Crusade.

AUGUST 1963 — Dr. Martin Luther King, Jr., gives his famous "I Have a Dream" speech at the March on Washington.

SEPTEMBER 1963 — A Ku Klux Klan bombing kills four girls going to Sunday school in Birmingham, Alabama.

JUNE 1964 — Freedom Summer volunteers register black voters in Mississippi.

JULY 1964 — The Civil Rights Act of 1964 supports school desegregation.

MARCH 1965 — Dr. Martin Luther King, Jr., joins a civil rights march from Selma to Montgomery, Alabama.

APRIL 1968 — Dr. Martin Luther King, Jr., is assassinated in Memphis, Tennessee.

1992 — The Brown v. Board of Education National Historic Site is established at Monroe Elementary School in Topeka, Kansas.

NOVEMBER 1999 — The Little Rock Nine are awarded the Congressional Gold Medal.

Photo Notes

Title page
Selma, Alabama, Mar. 1965
Civil rights activists hold hands
before marching to Montgomery.

Page 9
Washington, D.C., Mar. 1942
African American students read in a
segregated school.

Page 10
New Orleans, Louisiana
A segregated public school in New
Orleans.

Page 11
Uno, Virginia, Feb. 1947
A teacher reads to students in a
segregated school.

Page 13
West Virginia, 1962
A young African American girl plays
with a doll. During the *Brown v.
Board of Education* trial, an expert in
child development presented studies
done with children and dolls, which
showed that African American children identified
white skin as preferable to black skin.

Page 14
Athens, Alabama, ca. 1940s
A young boy sits in a school for
African American students.

Page 15
Georgia, ca. 1941
A rural segregated school.

Page 17
Topeka, Kansas, Jan. 1954
The daughters of Oliver Brown on
their route to school. Their father
joined a group of parents organized
by the NAACP to challenge the
Topeka school board to let their children go to
neighborhood schools rather than more distant
segregated schools. This Kansas lawsuit went to
the Supreme Court with similar cases from
Delaware, Virginia, South Carolina, and
Washington, D.C.

Page 20
New York City, May 18, 1954
The *New York Times* headline
announces the *Brown v. Board of
Education* decision.

Page 21
Washington, D.C., 1953
Members of the Supreme Court who
ruled in *Brown v. Board of Education*.
Seated from left to right: Felix
Frankfurter, Hugo L. Black, Earl
Warren, Stanley F. Reed, William O. Douglas.
Standing from left to right: Tom C. Clark, Robert H.
Jackson, Harold H. Burton, Sherman Minton.

Page 22 and front jacket
Fort Myer, Virginia, Sept. 1954
African American and white
children are together on the first
day of integration in their school.

Page 24
Washington, D.C., Sept. 1954
Students attend school together for
the first time in a formerly all-white
school.

Page 25
Washington, D.C., Sept. 1954
A teacher and students sit together in an integrated classroom after *Brown v. Board of Education.*

Page 26
Washington, D.C., Sept. 1954
Students run out for recess at an integrated school.

Page 27
Clinton, Tennessee, Aug. 1956
An angry mob tries to overturn a car with black passengers after being motivated by a speech against integration at the local high school.

Page 28
Clinton, Tennessee, Aug. 1956
Students protest desegregation at their high school, the first public school in Tennessee to integrate.

Page 29
Hillsboro, Oregon, Apr. 1956
A group of students and parents protest outside a segregated school. They had been turned away from the school for two years. The school district said it was waiting for official notice from the Supreme Court before taking action.

Page 30
Apr. 1956
Two children watch a Ku Klux Klan cross burn. The sign on the car protests integration.

Page 31
Englewood, New Jersey, Sept. 1962
African American students sit in a school boycotted by white students protesting its recent desegregation.

Page 33
Hutchins, Texas, Sept. 1954
A group of children with their parents stand outside a school that would not admit them because they were black. Though the Supreme Court ruled that segregated schools were illegal, Texas law made segregation compulsory at the time.

Page 34
Sturgis, Kentucky, Sept. 1957
On the fourth day of desegregation at a Kentucky high school, African American students walk through a crowd of white students jamming the school's entrance.

Page 35
Little Rock, Arkansas, Sept. 1957
Two of six African American students who attempted to integrate North Little Rock High School are jeered at as they try to enter the building.

Page 37
Little Rock, Arkansas, Sept. 1957
White students chase an African American student on the first day of integration at Central High School. Nine African American students planned to attend Central, until the governor disobeyed the Supreme Court ruling and ordered the Arkansas National Guard to prevent the students from entering the school. President Eisenhower intervened by sending one thousand paratroopers and ten thousand members of the National Guard to ensure the protection of the Little Rock Nine as they attended school.

Page 38
Little Rock, Arkansas, Sept. 1957
Members of the Arkansas National Guard turn Elizabeth Eckford away from Central High School.

Page 39
Little Rock, Arkansas, Sept. 1957
An angry crowd follows Elizabeth Eckford, one of the Little Rock Nine, as she tries to go to school.

Page 40
Little Rock, Arkansas, Oct. 1957
Elizabeth Eckford sits alone in the high school cafeteria. The Little Rock Nine attended school under the protection of federal troops.

Page 41
Little Rock, Arkansas, Sept. 1958
A black boy fights back when two white boys try to force his sister and him off the sidewalk while they are on their way to school.

Page 42
Virginia, 1958
Students attend a party to make school integration easier.

Page 43
Virginia, 1958
Two girls attend a party to prepare for school integration.

Page 44
New Orleans, Louisiana, Nov. 1960
Ruby Bridges attends first grade under U.S. Marshal escort. Ruby was the only black student at her school and the only child in her class, because many white parents took their children out of school to protest integration.

Page 45
New Orleans, Louisiana, Nov. 1960
Parents and teenagers protest against integration outside a local elementary school.

Page 46
Montgomery, Alabama, Sept. 1963
Students protest against desegregation ordered for Montgomery's schools by the Supreme Court.

Page 47
Queens, New York, Sept. 1959
Students enter their new school after being transferred. Hundreds of white students were kept home from school in a one-day boycott to protest the transfers.

Page 48
Huntsville, Alabama, Sept. 1963
A father walks his son to his first day of school at a formerly all-white school. Integration in Huntsville schools took place without incident.

Page 49
Dec. 1966
Students listen to a story in an integrated classroom.

Page 52
North Carolina, 1950
A man drinks from a segregated water fountain.

Page 53
Pensacola, Florida, 1930s
A movie theater in Florida has a separate back entrance for African Americans.

Page 54
New York City, May 1960
Picketers demand an end to segregation at lunch counters.

Page 55
Nashville, Tennessee, Mar. 1960
Two women sit at a lunch counter to protest segregation. Throughout

the country, black and white people staged sit-in protests. Often crowds tried to intimidate the protesters by staring and yelling at them and even pouring food and drinks on them. Sometimes the protesters were arrested.

Page 56
Washington, D.C., Aug. 1963
Black and white citizens travel to the March on Washington, a peaceful civil rights protest that attracted a crowd of more than 250,000 people.

Page 57
Cambridge, Maryland, July 1963
White and black protesters kneel on the sidewalk in front of a segregated restaurant and sing freedom songs. The owner of the restaurant broke raw eggs and poured water over their heads.

Page 58
Selma, Alabama, Mar. 1965
Civil rights activists marched from Selma to Montgomery to demand voting rights. This marcher wore a helmet for protection against state law enforcement officials who might try to stop the marchers.

Page 59
San Francisco, California, Apr. 1964
Demonstrators protest outside a hotel that refused to hire African American workers.

Page 61
Birmingham, Alabama, May 1963
A boy looks through a jail yard fence. He was arrested with hundreds of other young activists who marched for freedom and equality. City authorities attacked the demonstrators with police dogs and fire hoses. So many marchers were arrested that they clogged the local jails.

Page 63
Birmingham, Alabama, Dec. 1956
Rosa Parks sits on a Birmingham city bus one year after her refusal to give up her seat to a white passenger sparked the Montgomery bus boycott. African Americans walked and rode in carpools in protest of segregation on public buses for just over a year, until the Supreme Court banned segregation on city buses.

Page 64
Boston, Massachusetts, Apr. 1965
Dr. Martin Luther King, Jr., was a leader of the civil rights movement. He inspired many people to nonviolent protest through boycotts, marches, and demonstrations. Martin Luther King won the Nobel Peace Prize in 1964.

Page 65
Washington, D.C., Aug. 1963
Dr. Martin Luther King, Jr., addresses a large crowd of peaceful demonstrators at a march on Washington, during which he delivered his "I Have a Dream" speech.

Page 66 and 79
Chicago, Illinois, Sept. 1963
Students in this school integrated without any racial strife.

Page 67
Queens, New York, Sept. 1959
A black and a white student work with each other in an integrated school.

Page 68
Berkeley, California, Nov. 1971
White and black students eat lunch together in an integrated school.

Page 69
Washington, D.C., 1988 or 1989
A young boy draws on a blackboard.

Page 70 and back jacket
Boston, Massachusetts, Sept. 1975
Students hold hands on the bus ride to their integrated school after local unrest over using busing to desegregate the schools.

Page 72
Birmingham, Alabama, 1963
Denise McNair, Carole Robertson, Addie Mae Collins, and Cynthia Wesley were killed when a bomb set by racists exploded in the Sixteenth Street Baptist Church, where the girls attended Sunday school.